Will   Irma   Taranee   Cornelia   Hay Lin

SECRETS

HarperCollins *Children's Books*

First published in the USA by Volo/Hyperion Books for Children.

First published in Great Britain in 2006 by HarperCollins Children's Books.
HarperCollins Children's Books is a division of HarperCollins Publishers Ltd.

The HarperCollins Children's Books website is at
www.harpercollinschildrensbooks.co.uk

ISBN: 0-00-723266-7
ISBN-13: 978-000-723266-6

1 2 3 4 5 6 7 8 9 10

The HarperCollins Children's Books website is at
www.harpercollinschildrensbooks.co.uk

Printed and bound in Italy

Visit www.clubwitch.co.uk

CONTENTS

CHAPTER ONE
TOP SECRET!

FROM WILL'S DIARY

⑥ *Friday*

Secrets! Thank goodness for secrets! I was thinking about it this morning. What would happen if everyone knew that my four friends and I were . . . Guardians of the Veil? The kids at school would be like: "Will, since you have special powers, could you make all our teachers disappear from the face of the earth?" The temptation would be irresistible! "Will, I like Tom! Can you make him fall in love with me?" It would be nonstop torture! But, I have to admit: Having this secret is a great way to unite us. It's something special that makes us unique and indispensable to each other. We'd still be great friends anyway, but the secret we share has made us into a strong group.

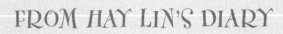

FROM HAY LIN'S DIARY

☽ *Monday*

Great news! I've finally discovered Lisa's secret! She's been buzzing around me in class and I couldn't figure out why. . . . But today she finally revealed that she really likes the way I draw. She saw a sketch of mine that I had left in my math notebook. And since she likes drawing clothes a lot, too, tomorrow afternoon I'm going over to her house. I'm glad she told me because we now share a secret dream: to become fashion designers. Now we can trade a whole bunch of useful information. We'll be sharing something that is only ours to share, and most of all, we'll have a blast together.

2

FROM CORNELIA'S DIARY

⑥ *Wednesday*

Secret. Private. Why do there have to be people who cannot understand these two simple words?! Take the Grumper sisters, for example. They managed to find out somehow that Kelly's violet-blue eyes are in reality not blue at all: she wears coloured contacts! As soon as they found out they blabbed the big news to everybody, so now the whole school knows.

Kelly was so embarrassed. So yesterday I decided to wear coloured contacts to school, too. During lunch everyone was amazed at my new, yellow cat eyes. They looked so cool that now half the school wants them! And the Grumper sisters were green with envy because all the kids started asking Kelly for advice.

Nobody has the right to get attention by revealing other people's secrets. Each of us has something that we don't want revealed . . . and we have the right to keep it secret and tell only the people that we trust. This concept, however, may be too much for those two snakes to grasp!

THE ORACLE SAYS ...

If our secrets are important to us, then other people's secrets are important to them. Try not to betray the trust of someone who has confided a secret in you. If you feel you're on the verge of doing so, stop and think how you felt the last time someone gave one of your secrets away.

DEAR IRMA

Irma likes to see the funny side of situations. Check out her response to these letters!

Dear Irma,
What should I do if my secret is found out?
– Found Out

Dear Found Out,
Invite it in . . . it might be freezing outside!
And keep your chin up.
♥ Irma

Dear Irma,
How can you tell when it's safe to reveal a secret?
– Not Sure

Dear Not Sure,
When you're sure the person you're telling
it to isn't a spy!
♥ Irma

Dear Irma,
I like a guy in my class. Should I keep it a secret?
– Crushing in Class

Dear Crushing,
No, because he may have the same little secret
about you, too. Don't be afraid to let your
feelings be known!
♥ Irma

Dear Irma,
Sometimes secrets can be hard to swallow.
What should I do?
– Nervous

Dear Nervous,
Try a tall glass of water!
♥ Irma

Dear Irma,
My mother wants me to tell her one of my
secrets each week. But I don't have that many!
– No Secrets

Dear No Secrets,
No problem: ask her if she'll accept repeats!
♥ Irma

FIVE TIPS ON KEEPING A SECRET – SECRET!

WILL: I change the password on my computer every Monday.

IRMA: Secret? I don't know what you're talking about!

TARANEE: I keep my secret in the safest place I know: my head!

CORNELIA: I write my secret in my diary, which then gets hidden.

HAY LIN: I write my secret on my hands. . . . in a secret code.

WHAT'S TOP SECRET?

❀ Something special to you.

❀ A friend trusting you with her secret.

❀ Knowing a secret about a friend or someone in your family.

❀ Giving a surprise party or gift.

❀ And sometimes, knowing you don't want to share. Your thoughts are **Top Secret!**

CHAPTER TWO
KEEP OUT!

⑥ *Thursday afternoon*

Peter's room

Peter: Taranee! What are you doing in here?

Taranee: Ahem . . . hi, Peter! I . . .

Peter: Give me that letter! You know you shouldn't be going through my stuff!

Taranee: But I was just looking for . . .

Peter: Out!

Taranee: Wait! Let me explain. . . .

Peter: I said . . . OUT!!!

Taranee calls Cornelia for an emergency consultation.

Cornelia: What's up? Trouble brewing?

Taranee: I guess so. . . . And it's all because of a stupid CD!

Cornelia: What are you talking about? I don't understand.

Taranee: Today I went into Peter's room to look for a CD that I lent him. He wasn't around, so I had to go through the mess on his desk. . . .

Cornelia: If his desk is anything like mine, it must have taken forever for you to find it.

7

Taranee: No kidding! And the worst part was, I didn't find my CD. But I did find all his letters from Miriam.

Cornelia: **Who's that?**

Taranee: A girl we met at the beach last summer. I think she has a crush on Peter. She keeps sending him long letters with little hearts drawn on them.

Cornelia: **How do you know?**

Taranee: Well . . . I peeked! And I had one in my hands when Peter walked in. He was so mad!

Cornelia: **I bet. I get mad whenever I catch Lilian snooping through my stuff!**

Taranee: Wait a minute! I wasn't snooping! I just happened to come across those letters. I didn't do it on purpose.

Cornelia: **I know, but that doesn't change matters much. When he caught you in his room reading one of his letters, Peter must have figured you weren't respecting his privacy.**

Taranee: But it's not like our house is some top-secret experimental laboratory where you need a written permit to go from one room to the next! Besides, I thought there were no secrets between Peter and me.

Cornelia: **Keeping something to yourself isn't a**

crime, you know. . . . whether it's a letter or a sticker! And your room is your territory, where you have the right to keep things that are important to you – and private!

Taranee: Maybe you're right, but I didn't think Peter would react like that. I mean, I've been in his room lots of times.

Cornelia: I know, but the difference is, you didn't have permission! Peter can let you in, but without that permission, you're invading his space. You're snooping!

Taranee: I guess you're right. I should have waited until Peter came home and then asked him for the CD. And I guess I shouldn't have read that letter.

Cornelia: Don't take it so hard! I'm sure you two will make up soon.

Taranee: I guess so – especially if I apologise with a pint of ice cream!

Cornelia: Good idea! And maybe some day he'll show you the letters from Miriam. . . .

Taranee: That's highly unlikely!

Cornelia: Maybe . . . but if he does, will you tell me what they say?

Taranee: CORNELIA! After everything you said about respecting privacy.

THE ORACLE SAYS . . .

Your room is your own private world, and it's completely natural for you to want to defend it from raids by family members.

The best "strategy" is to act toward others as you expect others to act toward you. Try setting an example: for instance, always ask your brothers or sisters before you borrow their things, and remember to knock before entering their rooms. That way you can expect the same respect from them.

DEAR TARANEE
Taranee loves to read and to have a good time. Her responses to these letters are thoughtful and funny!

Dear Taranee,
Why does my sister consider herself top dog in our room?
– Lil' Sister

Dear Lil' Sister,
Maybe because she sleeps in the top bunk! It might help if you talk to her honestly. Maybe she doesn't realise how she makes you feel.
❋ Taranee

Dear Taranee,
My mother says I can't hang up posters of my
favourite stars in my room. What can I do?
– Star-Mad

Dear Star-Mad,
Ask if you can hang them up in *her* room! She might
get annoyed at that . . . so maybe try asking if you
can hang one poster and see if she lets you.
✳ Taranee

Dear Taranee,
My mother is constantly rearranging the furniture in
my room. Is she trying to find out where I hide my
secrets?
– Feeling Invaded

Dear Feeling Invaded,
No, but maybe she's harboring a secret desire to
become an interior decorator! You should tell her
what you like and see if you can work together.
✳ Taranee

Dear Taranee,
My sister always has her hands in my stuff. What
can I do?
– Hands Off

Dear Hands Off,
Cheer up, it would be worse it she had her *feet* in
your stuff! Explain that your stuff is off limits.
✳ Taranee

WHAT CAN YOU DO IF . . .

You want a space all your own but you share your room with a brother or sister?

- Join forces. It will be easier to defend your privacy with an ally.
- Agree on a set of rules that will help you both get along, even if it means making a few compromises.
- Divide the room into two zones, leaving the path to the door as a neutral area.

You suspect that someone has been going through your things?

- To find out if someone has been snooping, set little traps: hide a pencil among your papers or a nearly invisible thread among your clothes, and remember their exact position. If you find them out of place upon return, you know someone has been snooping.
- Catch the snooper off guard by placing embarrassing notes inside your hiding places, with messages like: "What do you think you're doing, poking around in my stuff?"

• Place a tape recorder on your desk and press the record button when you go out. You'll be able to find out whether someone has come in or not when you play the tape back.

Everyone just barges into your room without knocking?

• Have a family meeting and ask that your space be respected as yours.
• Hang a sign on the door with large block letters that say KNOCK BEFORE ENTERING.
• Hang a bell in the doorway. It will warn you when someone's coming in.

WILL'S TIPS

My room is my own little world where I can . . .

- Daydream as much as I want.
- Talk and laugh for hours with my friends.
- Hide my most secret and precious objects.
- Listen to my favourite song fifteen times in a row.
- Cover the walls with pictures of my friends.
- Surround myself with posters of my favourite stars.
- Light candles (with permission).
- Keep out anyone I want to!

CHAPTER THREE
SEEKING REFUGE

⑥ *Saturday afternoon*

Heatherfield Mall

Cornelia: **Strange that Taranee didn't want to come shopping with us – I'm worried about her.**

Irma: What's so strange about it?

Cornelia: **I want to be sure that everything's okay.**

Will: It *is* strange. She told me she wanted to go out by herself. That's not like her!

Hay Lin: **Maybe she just wanted some alone time. There's nothing wrong with that.**

Will: It's just that we usually hang out together, that's all.

Hay Lin: **I know, but sometimes being alone is a good way to clear your head.**

Irma: You're right, Hay Lin. And sometimes holing up in your room just doesn't cut it.

Cornelia: **Especially when you've got a hurricane like my little sister around!**

Hay Lin: I don't have that problem, but on some days my room is definitely too small.

Irma: **Mine, too. Sometimes I could lie on my bed for hours listening to music, but there are other times when I get bored.**

Will: **So what do you do?**

Irma: I put on my headphones and take a walk in the park. Sometimes I get so into it that I start singing at the top of my lungs.

Cornelia: **And you're probably the only one in the park who's enjoying that!**

Irma is about to respond, but Hay Lin manages to stop her in time.

Hay Lin: Take it easy, girls.

Will: **Yeah, knock it off. As you were saying . . .**

Irma: Going out by yourself can be great.

Hay Lin: **Yeah, like, whenever I have to make an important decision, I always go to my secret spot.**

Irma, Will, and Cornelia (together): Secret spot?

Hay Lin: **Yeah, sort of . . . well, let me explain, but promise not to laugh.**

Irma: We would never laugh . . . GUARDIAN'S HONOUR!

Hay Lin: **I go to the Heatherfield Museum. There is a painting that I really love. So I go and sit in front of it, look at it . . . and it really gets me thinking.**

16

Will: That's kind of like when I go to the pool. It's
            time for myself, to think, to relax. . . .
            Swimming helps me feel better, especially
            after I have an argument with my mum.

Cornelia: **I do the same thing with ice-skating!**

Irma: You see? We all have our own secret spot, a
            magical place where we can go whenever we
            need to.

Hay Lin: **That's why we shouldn't be insulted or
            worry about the fact that Taranee didn't
            come with us today.**

Irma: At this point, I propose an agreement. . . .

Cornelia: **What kind of agreement?**

Hay Lin: That we promise never to feel betrayed or
            neglected if one of us chooses to spend a
            little time on her own.

Irma, Will, **and** Cornelia **(together): It's a deal!**

Just then Taranee shows up.

Taranee: **Hey! What's going on?**

Irma: Well, we've got lots to tell you, but first you
            tell us: how was the photo shoot?

Cornelia: **I can't wait till you get the pictures
            developed!**

Hay Lin: Where did you go to take them?

Taranee: **Wow! I didn't know you girls were so
            interested! I thought you'd be mad because
            I wasn't coming with you. . . .**

Irma, Will, and Cornelia smile knowingly at one another.

DEAR CORNELIA
Laugh your doubts away with Cornelia!

Dear Cornelia,
I want to build my own secret tree house. Any
advice?
– Seeking Secret Place

Dear Seeking,
Great idea. But choose your tree well. If you plan
on using your tree house for sad moments, try a
weeping willow. If you want to keep it your own
little secret . . . a bonsai tree works best!
❀ Cornelia

Dear Cornelia,
At the park I have my own bench, but the last time
I went there somebody was sitting on it!
– Bummed

Dear Bummed,
If you don't want other people to sit there, try
hanging a WET PAINT sign on it!
❀ Cornelia

Dear Cornelia,
My friends get insulted if I don't go out with
them. What should I do?
– No Time Alone

Dear No Time Alone,
It's perfectly normal to want to be alone
sometimes. Remember that true friends

respect your need to be alone. After all, spending time alone helps you to recharge your batteries, which is a benefit to both you and your friends!
❀ Cornelia

Dear Cornelia,
I want a special spot where I can go and hang out by myself. But where?
– X Spot

Dear X Spot,
It's easy. Normally, the best spot for you is where you feel most comfortable. Try wandering around going nowhere in particular, and you may just stumble across that magical place in your own backyard, local park, or even at school!
❀ Cornelia

Dear Cornelia,
My friends want to come and share my secret place. I don't want them to!
– Hidden Secret

Dear Hidden Secret,
Don't feel obliged to share your secret. Invite your friends only if you really want them to come. Try to make them understand that your spot is just that . . . *yours.* Maybe help your friends find places of their own!
❀ Cornelia

SECRET SPOTS

- The balcony or patio. A little sun always helps recharge the batteries!

- The gym, because a good workout helps clear my thoughts!

- The library, where "Silence, please!" means I can think in peace!

- The mall, because getting lost in the crowd helps me find myself.

- Dance class, where concentrating on my moves means I can take a break from everything else.

CHAPTER FOUR
WE'VE ALL GOT A
D.L.H.W.I.
(DON'T LEAVE HOME WITHOUT IT)

FROM HAY LIN'S DIARY

◎ *Monday*
Yippee! Double yippee! An internship at a
fashion institute in Paris for the summer!
I can't believe it! Now I know I'm going to
become a great designer. I'm so excited I can
hardly believe it!

◎ *Tuesday*
Uh-oh. Paris is not looking good. My
parents went to school for a conference
with my teachers. . . . and found out
I'm barely passing French! They said
that with such a low grade level of
French comprehension, the internship
would be a waste of time. I begged

them, I pleaded. . . . but it was no use – they refused to listen.

⑥ *Wednesday*

I made a deal with my parents: I promised them that if they let me go to Paris, I'd get a good grade on the French final. I know I can do it, I have to do it, even if it means locking myself in my room to study, day and night!

This is it. I've reviewed everything: irregular verbs, conjunctions, etc. I only wish someone else could take the test in my place! My backpack is all ready for school tomorrow. . . . I've even got my good-luck charm, an ancient Chinese coin my grandmother gave me. I always bring it whenever I have to do something important and need good luck.

⑥ *Thursday*

What a day! When I got to school I put my hand in my pocket to make sure the coin was there, but it was gone! I must have turned pale as a ghost, because Taranee immediately asked what was wrong. Wrong? Everything! I felt completely *lost* without my good-luck charm. But I couldn't tell anyone what was going on because:

    1. Good-luck charms lose their power once someone else finds out.

    2. I didn't know whether the others would understand, and at the time I had no desire to give any explanations. Of course, it doesn't make much sense to hope an old coin can bring good luck, though you never know. . . .

    Anyhow, I began the test with my fingers crossed, repeating over and over again that I had studied and was as prepared as could be.

    We get the tests back next week: I don't know if I can wait!

⑤ Saturday

I found the coin! I had put it in my backpack pocket, and not in my jacket pocket – which means that I did have it with me while I took the test. I wonder if it did any good. Last month I had my good-luck charm with me for my history oral. Only I hadn't studied a bit. . . . and I totally bombed!

⑤ Monday

Woo-hoo! I got the highest grade in the class!

Paris, here I come!!! Wow! I actually did it! My parents have already confirmed my spot for the internship.

Even my friends were surprised and congratulated me. They did, however, ask me about my strange behaviour before the test. When I told them that I had been worried about losing my good-luck charm they burst out laughing – but not because they thought it was silly.

No – and this is the incredible thing – they were shocked that I thought they wouldn't understand. As it turns out, they've each got their own good-luck charm, too!

It's okay to keep your good-luck charm a secret. Just make sure that you do everything in your power to make sure good luck is always on your side!

THE ORACLE SAYS . . .

We can create good luck by believing in what we do. If you're optimistic and face up to your difficulties, you'll find that the true magic lies within you. Your strength and desire to succeed are far greater than you might believe. This knowledge is the real good-luck charm that you should always carry with you!

SECRET TIPS

Good-luck charms – you can have more than one!

WILL: I hug my dormouse.
IRMA: I eat lots of chocolate.
TARANEE: I blast my favourite song on the stereo.
CORNELIA: I never go out without my bracelet.
HAY LIN: I carry my favourite paintbrush in my back pocket.

CHAPTER FIVE
HANDS OFF!

⑥ Tuesday afternoon

Cornelia: Irma, you look bummed! Bad day?

Irma: The worst!

Taranee: What happened?

Irma: Oh, it's just awful.

Will: Do you want to talk about it?

Irma: Sure, even if there's nothing we can do about it now. . . .

Hay Lin: Come on, let's hear it!

Irma: Remember the pen that Nate lent me?

Hay Lin: Nate the hottie? That wonderful, sweet –

Taranee: We get the message, Hay Lin!

Irma: Yes! Him!

Cornelia: Ah, and if I remember correctly, it was the pen you just *happened* to borrow when you just *happened* to walk into class to find out if someone just *happened* to know when Mr.Collins's free period was –

Irma: Will you just let me tell the story already?

Taranee:	Oh, sorry – go right ahead.
Irma:	Well . . . you know how important that pen was to me. I mean, after going to all that trouble to get it, I didn't even bring it to school, because I was afraid of losing it!
Will:	I thought you wanted to keep it in order to have an excuse to talk to Nate!
Irma:	That, too! But now, I can't even do that. Yesterday, my brother was home sick. He wandered into my room, saw the pen, and took it!
Taranee:	And that's it?
Irma:	I wish! But the lughead broke it and my mum threw it away!
Hay Lin:	Your family is clearly plotting against you!
Taranee:	I know what you mean! I can hardly keep anything in my house without *somebody* getting their hands on it. Forget secrets, I mean *anything* that's important to me. My mother's worse than a vacuum cleaner: anything she finds that she doesn't think is important, she throws out.
Will:	You have to find a special place to put your special or important things. A kind of secret hiding place. Your own private treasure chest!

Cornelia: You're right. That's what I ended up doing to keep my sister out of my stuff. I keep my most precious things locked in a box, which I keep hidden in the back of my drawer.

Taranee: Does it work? What about your parents?

Cornelia: They don't suspect a thing! But that means I have to keep my room neat. Then my mum won't have an excuse to go in and straighten up.

Irma: You've got your work cut out for you!

Will: Yeah, but it's worth it!

Irma: Okay, girls . . . I've got to get home!

Will: What's wrong now?

Irma: Nothing! I just decided to become extreeeemely neat and tidy!

Cornelia: Ha! And tomorrow we want a detailed report on everything you put in your secret box!

Irma: No problem – as long as you tell me what's in yours first!

Cornelia: Well, in exchange I could offer you an interesting bit of information. . . .

Irma: Like?

Cornelia: Like . . . Nate approaching, at twelve o'clock!

Irma: Honey, my secrets are yours! Bye!

DEAR HAY LIN
Ask Hay Lin what to do.
She gives great and
cheerful responses!

Dear Hay Lin,
I've lost the key to my secret box. How can I get
a copy?
– Lost Key

Dear Lost,
Ask your friend the copycat! See if you can pick
the lock with a pin or take the box to a
locksmith.
:butterfly: Hay Lin

Dear Hay Lin,
I hid my crush's pictures in my sock drawer. Is that
a good hiding place?
– Keeping Secrets

Dear Keeping Secrets,
Sure, if those pictures really sock it to you! That
seems like the perfect hiding place.
:butterfly: Hay Lin

Dear Hay Lin,
Is my bed a good hiding place for my secrets?
– Sleepy

Dear Sleepy,
Yes, as long as you don't have any bedbugs!
:butterfly: Hay Lin

FIVE TIPS ON WHERE TO HIDE A SECRET LETTER

WILL: E-mail! Nobody knows my password but me!

IRMA: Inside my Karmilla CD case, underneath the cover.

TARANEE: Inside my photo album of insects. Nobody in my family likes bugs!

CORNELIA: Under the false bottom of my jewelry box.

HAY LIN: Inside the folder where I keep my drawing rejects. The pictures may be awful, but they sure are useful!

TARANEE'S TIPS

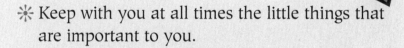

Hiding your secrets

❋ Keep with you at all times the little things that are important to you.

❋ Don't hide all your treasures in just one place. Spread them around.

❋ Make a fake secret box to throw snoopers off the trail, and keep it in an obvious place.

❋ Place the secret item in an envelope and the envelope inside a pencil case, the pencil case inside a bag, the bag inside a closet, and so on. People will lose patience before they can find the object.

❋ Keep your secret stuff in perfect order, and memorize it. The slightest disorder means someone has been snooping.

CHAPTER SIX
WHY ME?

FROM WILL'S DIARY

🌀 *Thursday*

I can't take it anymore! My mum's done it again – I've pleaded with her a hundred times not to call me Wilma!

And in front of Uriah and his gang! I can't believe it. I can just imagine the teasing I'm going to get at school tomorrow: "Wilma! Oh, Wilma!" HELP!

I keep reliving the moment over in my mind: I'm helping my mother load shopping bags into the car, and there they are, laughing as they look on, saying, "What a good girl, Will! Helping Mummy." So I go over to give them a piece of my mind, and there's my mum calling, "Wilma, come on! It's late!" Oh, I wish I could disappear from the face of the earth! Or at least wear a bag over my head at school tomorrow!

⑥ *Thursday night*

Talking to Cornelia on the phone made me feel
better. She told me about something that
happened a while ago. She had some classmates
over for a study group, and while they were
having their snack, Lilian appeared, waving a
picture Cornelia had put up in her room of a boy
she had a crush on.

She said she turned every shade of red
imaginable (I believe it!) and that afterward she
started blabbering ridiculous things like, "I was
practicing for art class. . . ." and so on. The kids
couldn't stop laughing at her. In the end, she
realised that it wasn't worth trying to come up
with excuses, and that in reality that just made
things worse. What it comes down to is: the best
way to walk out of a situation with your head
held high is to just play along with it, take it as a
joke, and not get uptight about it – because
people who tease you delight in seeing you
squirm. The best way to defend yourself from a
practical joke is to laugh at yourself; that way,
the people teasing you realise they can't do you
any harm, and the joke ends then and there.

Of course, that's easier said than done (especially if you've got a personality like Cornelia's!), but at least I should give it a TRY!

✪ Friday

Incredible! It worked! As predicted, as soon as Uriah and his crew saw me, they started in with "Wilma, Wilma!" When I heard them, it made my blood boil. . . . I was actually tempted to run and hide, but I remembered Cornelia's story. So I turned around and smiled, and said, ever so sweetly, "Why, boys, it's such a pleasure to see you!" They couldn't believe it! They looked at me openmouthed, not knowing what to say beyond a very shy and embarrassed "Hi, Will."

I knew I could do it!

⑥ *Saturday*

Today I had a little talk with my mum. I couldn't keep quiet any longer. And, wouldn't you know it, she was the one who left me with my mouth hanging open! When I told her I was embarrassed at being called Wilma in front of the other kids, she said that she understood and would try to start just calling me Will. Then she said she was glad I was being honest with her! I told her that I was happy to have such an "original" name. Only, if we could keep it a secret, it would be all the more special.

DEAR WILL

Advice from the Keeper of the Heart of Candracar! Will knows the deal and is ready to share!

Dear Will,
My classmates tease me because they saw the phrase Dopey, I love you *written in my notebook. But Dopey is my dog. . . .*
– Puppy Love

Dear Puppy Love,
So what? Now they think that you have a boyfriend who is a real dream!
🐸 Will

Dear Will,
My mother came to pick me up at school dressed exactly like me. I wanted to run and hide. . . .
– Seeing Double

Dear Seeing Double,
Why were *you* so badly dressed? Think of it as a compliment.
🐸 Will

Dear Will,
My brother told my friends that he saw me holding
hands with a boy. What should I do?
– Caught Red-handed

Dear Caught,
Take him to have his eyes examined, since he
missed seeing you two hugging. Don't worry
about what he says. But you should tell your
friends what's going on. They'll be happy for you!
🐸 Will

OOPS! THAT COULD BE EMBARRASSING. . . .

🍀 You're at a party and realise you are wearing the same thing as the host.

🍀 You've just finished talking to your crush. . . . and then you realise you have food in your teeth!

🍀 Just as you are walking by the cutest boy in the school, you trip and fall, and all your books go flying!

Whenever you do something slightly
embarrassing, the best thing to do is
laugh it off: it could happen to anybody!

CHAPTER SEVEN
HOLD THAT TONGUE!

⑥ *Saturday afternoon*

Will, Cornelia, and Taranee in Taranee's room

Cornelia: Hey, Taranee – baggy T-shirt, extra-large sweats – is this some new fashion statement?

Will: We've got a feeling you want to stay in here for good.

Taranee: That's right. I'm not setting foot outside as long as I live. I want to disappear!

Cornelia: Be careful what you wish for – you never know what will happen, with our powers!

Will: A quick shower and a new outfit could solve everything.

Taranee: This is no laughing matter. Hay Lin is never going to speak to me again. And I don't blame her!

Cornelia: What did you do? Whatever it is, it can't be that bad!

Will: Come on, spill the beans.

Taranee: Today Mrs. Rudolph gave us a

makeup math quiz, and Hay Lin blew it big-time. We were discussing it during lunch, when Alex showed up. . . .

Cornelia: Oh, no! She is such a gossip queen!

Taranee: Yeah, but I wasn't thinking. . . . So, when she came by, I told her how things had gone, including about Hay Lin's bad grade!

Cornelia: I can just imagine Alex's reaction. . . .

Taranee: It wasn't pretty!

Will: What about Hay Lin? Did she get mad?

Taranee: She should have. But no, she just stood there and took it. Then when Alex left, she walked back into class without even looking at me.

Will: Did you try to apologise?

Taranee: I wanted to, but I didn't know what to say. . . . I really messed up.

Will: Well, you'd better think of something quick.

Taranee: But I can't!

Cornelia: Wrong! Come on, put on your jeans. Hurry up.

A half hour later, the three girls are in the park.

Will: Go on, go say something.

Taranee: But I can't!

Cornelia: Listen, Taranee. . . . You didn't mean to give away Hay Lin's secret, but now you should apologise. . . . It will be better in the long run. If you don't talk it over, you may lose her trust for good. Saying you're sorry isn't easy, but I think friendship is worth it.

Will: **Cornelia's right. Hay Lin is your friend. She'll understand.**

Taranee: Okay. I'll give it a shot.

Irma and Hay Lin walk over.

Irma: **Hi! You're late!**

Hay Lin: Hi.

Taranee: **Hay Lin, can I talk to you for a minute – alone?**

Irma: Why alone? Are you telling secrets?

Will: **Leave it alone, Irma.**

Hay Lin and Taranee go off for a little talk.

Taranee: Listen, Hay Lin, I don't know where to begin. Um . . . I just wanted to say that . . . I'm sorry. Secrets are meant to be kept, and today, at school, I totally blew it.

Hay Lin: **I know you didn't do it on purpose. But all the same, I'm glad you apologised.**

Taranee: Do you still trust me?

Hay Lin: **Sure I do! Just remember not to blab to the whole school next time I get a bad grade!**

Taranee: You got it!

Meanwhile, off to the side . . .

Irma: **Why can't I listen in?**

Will: **They'll tell you about it later!**

Irma: **Well, since you guys keep me in the dark about everything, maybe I shouldn't tell you that Matt is down at the skating rink this very minute!**

Will: **WHAT?**

Cornelia: **Hay Lin! Taranee! Get a move on! Will suddenly has an irresistible desire to go skating!**

HAY LIN'S TIPS

Golden rules for keeping a secret

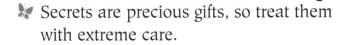

🦋 Secrets are precious gifts, so treat them with extreme care.

🦋 Don't tell someone else's secret – it's a sign of disrespect.

🦋 Be careful – "secretly" divulging someone else's secret can backfire – fast.

🦋 A secret usually gets distorted as it gets spread around, to the point where it can actually become a lie. Keep secrets secret!

TEST

See how discreet you are.

1. There's a new girl in class. Your reaction is . . .
   A. Let's hope she's nice!
   B. I wonder why she moved?
   C. Oh, really?

2. One of your classmates has been absent for a while and you don't know why.
   A. Something's not right. You call her to see if something's happened.
   B. You ask your classmates if they've heard anything.
   C. Who cares? You never liked her anyway.

3. You overhear two classmates arguing in the hall.
   A. You go over with your friend the black belt.
   B. You go on your way and tell a friend later.
   C. You don't approach – it's their business, not yours.

4. You find a classmate's datebook on the floor next to the teacher's desk.
   A. You pick it up and see whose it is.

B. You snag it – It'll make for good reading later!

C. You leave it where it is.

5. You catch a classmate looking through your backpack.

    A. Taken aback, you ask the person what she or he is looking for.

    B. You begin hurling every insult you know at the person.

    C. You're not bothered; you've got nothing to hide.

6. You hear that Lisa, who always gets excellent marks, is a big cheat. You . . .

    A. Already knew it, but why gossip about it?

    B. Run and tell the teacher.

    C. Ignore it: after all, she's not the only one who does it, is she?

7. You see a friend's boyfriend giving a present to another girl. How do you react?

    A. You don't do anything, but you keep an eye on him. You never know.

    B. Since you know the girl, you try to find out what he gave her.

    C. You can't be bothered. That's their business!

8. One of your classmates hasn't spoken to you in a month. You . . .
   - A. Ask what the matter is.
   - B. Don't say anything, but ask around to see what's up.
   - C. Hadn't even realised!

PROFILES

You answered mostly A.

Little Miss Discreet

Your secret-finder radar is as efficient and on-the-mark as ever, but you know when it's better to lay off and not get tangled up in other people's affairs. You're smart enough not to believe everything you hear, and you'd rather go directly to the source to get the real story. You demand the same respect you give others. Unfortunately, you risk running into others who don't act as you do, so choose your confidants with care. Other than that, don't change a thing!

You answered mostly B.

Curiosity Killed the Cat

Being discreet? You don't let that get in the

way of your inner curiosity. You're the one likely to butt right into other people's business. In every situation there lurk mystery and allure, and you've got your antennae poised for reception. But beware: your actions have consequences. Imagine you had a secret to keep and some busybody like yourself kept bugging you!

You answered mostly *C*.

Who Cares?

Your motto is: It's none of my business! You couldn't care less about other people's tidbits of info – their lives don't mean that much to you, anyway. You are much more interesting than anybody else. When someone's talking to you, you don't even realise the person's speaking because you're busy thinking about what you're going to do next Wednesday afternoon.

A Dead Heat.

Have you scored, for example, three *A*'s and three *B*'s? Then you're a mixture of both types. Sometimes it depends on the situation. . . . being discreet takes practise!

CHAPTER EIGHT
STRENGTH IN NUMBERS

⑤ *Monday morning*

Sheffield Institute

Cornelia: Hi, Will! You look like you're in a good mood.

Will: Yes!

Cornelia: What's up?

Will: You won't believe it, but this morning when I walked into class, I found a note on my desk . . . signed with a great big *M*! Matt invited me for some ice cream after school today.

Cornelia: Really? That's amazing!

Will: I know! I was so happy I wanted to start whooping and hollering, right there in front of everybody!

Just then Irma comes running up.

Cornelia: Hey, is everything okay?

Irma: No! I've been looking for you. . . . It's a Grumper emergency!

Will: What have they done this time?

Irma: You're meeting Matt today, right?

Will's expression suddenly changes.

Will: **How did you know?**

Irma: That's the emergency I'm talking about.

Cornelia: **Hey, what's going on?**

Irma: This morning I overheard the Grumper sisters whispering in the girls' room. . . . Will, they read the note, and they plan on following you so they can find out who your mystery date is!

Will: **Oh, no! How am I supposed to have fun with Matt if those two are around?**

Irma: Let's ask Hay Lin and Taranee for help.

Cornelia: **Yes! They'll have a solution!**

Will: Come on. We have to hurry!

The three girls meet up with Hay Lin and Taranee, and fill them in on all the latest news.

Hay Lin: **Those Grumper sisters . . . what a royal pain!**

Taranee: There's only one way to keep those two busybodies out of this: while Will goes to meet Matt, we can throw them off the trail. I've already got a plan in mind. . . .

Irma: **Shouldn't Will get back to class now? If the Grumper sisters see us**

all plotting together, they might get suspicious!

Will: You're right. But let's meet up after school to find out how everything goes!

Later, the five of them meet at their usual park bench.

Taranee: How'd it go, Will?

Will: Great! Matt and I spent two amazing hours together. . . . and all thanks to you! You are the best friends a girl could have!

Irma: Well, let's just say our afternoon was somewhat less amazing.

Taranee: Operation Grumper worked like a charm!

Will: Come on, tell me everything!

Irma: As soon as the bell rang, I delayed the little snoops with a long-winded review of Karmilla's latest video. Then they tried to shake me by saying they had better things to do, but Taranee, Hay Lin, and Cornelia sprang into action.

Taranee: Hay Lin and I pretended to get into a fight because she didn't want to tell me one of her extremely important secrets.

Cornelia: And I tried to get them to cool it.

Hay Lin: The Grumper sisters couldn't resist, especially when Cornelia got them involved.

Will: Then what happened? Come on . . . the suspense is killing me!

Taranee: Hay Lin invited us *all* over to her house to talk things over. Now that was something the Grumper sisters couldn't pass up.

Will: What happened at Hay Lin's?

Irma: We talked for an hour about Hay Lin's secret as if it were the most important thing in the world – of course, without letting the cat out of the bag.

Taranee: With the Grumper sisters dying of curiosity!

Cornelia: It was hilarious! And after going over and over our oaths of secrecy, Hay Lin looked as if she were ready to spill the beans. . . . but in the end she changed her mind, leaving the Grumper sisters in the dark.

Hay Lin: We had them going the whole afternoon, hinting at a secret that in reality . . . never existed in the first place!

Taranee: While YOUR secret, Will, remained safe.

Will: You're the greatest!

Taranee: And speaking of sharing secrets, Will, you still haven't told us about your afternoon with Matt!

Will: Oh . . . he told me all about these new kittens at the pet shop. Maybe it doesn't sound like anything special to you, but . . .

Irma: Just spending time with him was special enough, right?

Will: You know me too well!

FIVE WAYS TO LET YOUR FRIENDS KNOW YOU'VE GOT A SECRET EMERGENCY

WILL: I sneeze three times in a row.

IRMA: I sing my favourite song, but change the words.

TARANEE: I take my glasses off and put them back on twice in a row.

CORNELIA: I move my good-luck bracelet from my left wrist to my right.

HAY LIN: I twist a lock of my hair.

THE ORACLE SAYS . . .

Sharing your secrets with good friends will lighten your burden. You should be able to trust your friends and know that they will guard your secrets as if they were their own.

CHAPTER NINE
WHO CAN I TELL?

FROM HAY LIN'S DIARY

☺ Monday

Incredible . . . Here I am at the beach with
something totally special to tell someone, only I
don't have anyone to tell. Maybe I should dig a
hole in the sand and yell my news into it – at
least I'd get it out of my system. I wish Will,
Taranee, Irma, and Cornelia were here! But that's
impossible, so I guess I'll have to trust some
friends from here. There's Kerry, Denise, Katia,
Elise, and John. Let's see. . . .

Kerry: No way! Her life is one big manicure. If I
told her I broke my leg, she'd probably
say she broke her nail. Of course, if
I needed advice on buying nail
polish, she'd be the person to ask.

Denise: She's everybody's friend . . . too friendly, actually. If I happened to tell her I'm thinking about cutting my hair, the next day the whole world would know the exact length, style, and colour I've decided on. With a friend like her, it's best to keep your mouth shut.

Katia: Little Miss Know-It-All. She's already seen and done everything, understands how everything works, is up on all the latest. The problem is . . . she never listens. I can just imagine our conversation. I'd say, "I've got this problem, and I don't know what to do." And she'd say, "You did the right thing by coming to me. I remember one time I had the same – " I'd say, "But I haven't even told you what it's about. See, there's this guy . . ." She'd say, "Oh, yeah, me, too. . . .When I first met Edwin . . ." Not a chance. Katia's out, too.

Elisa: She's nice, and I've never seen or heard about her betraying a friend. The only thing is, she just doesn't seem that interested in guys right now. I don't know if she would understand my dilemma.

John: No way. He's a boy. And he's also a good

friend of Rob's, and that's who my secret's about.

So as it turns out, I've got two choices: either I don't say anything to anybody, or I try telling Elisa.

She could be the right person. The fact that we're not interested in the same things shouldn't be a problem. After all, if she's as on the ball and sensitive as she appears to be, she'll know how to put herself in my shoes and come up with some advice for me.

⑥ *Wednesday*

Yikes! It worked! At last I've gotten this big secret of mine off my chest! I told Elisa that Rob wanted to ask me out, and she was so great about it. . . .

She listened to everything I had to say without interrupting me, which helped me to get some of my thoughts straight.

I didn't really want to spend a lot of time alone with Rob, although I didn't want to give him an absolute NO, either. She told me to make a date with him, promising that at a certain point she'd "just happen to" come strolling by and check up on us. So we decided she would find us on the beach, and we'd take it from there. What a fun night! All three of us ended up going for ice cream together! Then, on the way home, Elisa told me she liked John. And tomorrow, when we go to see Rob and John's diving competition, we won't have to worry about whom to talk to!

THE ORACLE SAYS . . .

Generally it's a good idea to entrust your secrets only to the people you know well. Friends who are good listeners and don't pass judgment before hearing all the facts are ideal, as are people who don't feel the need to attract attention to themselves by talking about your business to others.

Sometimes people you've just met inspire your trust right away, but remember: a bit of caution is always best in the beginning.

FIVE TIPS FOR FINDING SOMEONE WHO CAN KEEP A SECRET

WILL: I'm my own best confidante!

IRMA: I tell Leafy, my turtle!

TARANEE: Ha, that's another of my secrets!

CORNELIA: Make sure she's a good listener!

HAY LIN: I tell someone who doesn't bug me about wanting to hear all my secrets.

CHAPTER TEN
SOS PHONE BILL!

⑥ *Wednesday afternoon*

At the ice-cream store

Hay Lin: Irma, what's going on?

Cornelia: **Got the sudden irresistible urge for a double hot-fudge sundae?**

Irma: No, although I can feel it coming on, seeing as I'm about to be grounded for the next ten years. You know – one last wish.

Will: **You must really be in hot water!**

Irma: I am. I don't know just *how* hot yet.

Cornelia: **Come on . . . quit stalling!**

Taranee: Seriously! Tell us what's going on!

Irma: **Well . . . it's my phone bill!**

Hay Lin: Ohhh, that hurts.

Will: **But this month we've kept things under control! We've used the phone as little as possible, and only for emergency situations.**

Cornelia: So calling to ask me whether you should wear blue or yellow laces with your black shoes is an emergency situation?

Will: **Of course, because I was wearing grey**

pants and a blue sweatshirt. . . . and especially because I was on my way to the pet store, where I was bound to run into Matt!

Cornelia: Emergency or not, for us the telephone is a necessity. . . . How could we live without it?

Taranee: But my parents just don't understand. They say there's no reason to call each other all the time, since we see each other almost every day anyway.

Will: But it's not the same thing!

Hay Lin: So, Irma, about that bill?

Irma: I've got it right here! I took it and hid it when I found it in the mailbox. See how much damage I've done? I've got the feeling this is going to be a whopper!

Taranee: No, you'd better not open it – it might make your parents even angrier. The important thing now is to somehow soften the blow, so your parents don't cut off your phone privileges completely.

The girls eat their ice cream as they try to come up with a plan.

Hay Lin: I've got it! My folks get mad because they think I'm wasting money; they say I act . . .

Irma: . . . Irresponsible! That's exactly what mine say!

Hay Lin: So, the solution is obvious: all we have to do is act grown-up and responsible.

Irma: I don't get it. What are you talking about?

Hay Lin: All each of us has to do is set aside part of our allowances and, before our parents open the bill each month, give them the money we've saved, saying that it's only right that we contribute to paying the bill since we talk on the phone a lot.

Will: Hmmm . . . that might just work.

Cornelia: It's the only way, considering that we're the ones who are at fault!

Irma: But there's one problem: right now I'm flat broke!

Taranee: Don't worry, we'll help you. Remember, united we stand. . . .

Cornelia: . . . So come on, girls, let's fork it over!

And so the Emergency Telephone Fund is born. Thanks to everyone's contribution, Irma will have enough money to pay her part of her parents' phone bill.

Hay Lin: All agreed, then? Irma will be the first to test our new strategy. If everything goes according to our plan, each of us will be able to benefit the next time we rack up an outrageous phone bill.

Irma: Agreed! I'll call you girls to . . . oops, I mean, I'll tell you what happens tomorrow!

The next day . . .

Will: How'd you do?

Irma: When I offered to contribute, my father stood there speechless. When he finally snapped out of it, he admitted he'd never expected such a mature and responsible gesture on my part.

Cornelia: WOW! Mission accomplished!

Irma: You said it! And besides, it turned out that the bill was only about half of what the last bill had been. My parents wouldn't take the money I offered.

Taranee: So why don't we put it aside for future telephone emergencies?

Irma: Sounds good to me, but from now on, let's promise we won't stay on the phone for more than five minutes at a time.

Hay Lin: How about ten? Otherwise, we'll barely have enough time to say hi and bye!

Will: Okay, but we should limit our calls to no more than three a day.

Irma: Hmmm . . . why not four?

Will, Taranee:, Cornelia:, **and** Hay Lin **(together):** IRMA!!!

Irma: Oops, you're right. . . .

DEAR IRMA
Irma is the best at giving advice and a laugh!

Dear Irma,
I'm the only one I trust. Whom can I tell my secrets to?
– Alone

Dear Alone,
The mirror! Maybe try keeping a journal, so that you can record your secrets for yourself.
♥ Irma

Dear Irma,
There's a guy in my class I'm head over heels about! Whom can I tell?
– Falling Fast

Dear Falling Fast,
Well, to begin with . . . try telling the guy himself! Sometimes you need to give a guy a hint that you like him. Good luck!
♥ Irma

Dear Irma,
I told one of my secrets to half the world. Was that a mistake?
– Chatty

Dear Chatty,
It sure was: the other half of the world is still waiting to find out. . . . It's not a secret anymore if you tell everyone.
 Irma

Dear Irma,
I gave away a friend's secret in an English essay for school and she's furious. Why?
– Clueless

Dear Clueless,
Um . . . maybe because you made too many spelling mistakes! Or because you told her secret. Best to apologise and start keeping secrets better.
 Irma

SECRET TIPS

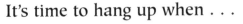

Use these "talkometers" to time your phone calls (and avoid those whopping bills!).

It's time to hang up when . . .

- ★ You've eaten five cookies.
- ★ The candle you lit has burned out.
- ★ You've covered your hand with scribbling.
- ★ The alarm that you set before calling rings.
- ★ A CD that you put on has finished.
- ★ You hear the ending theme song of the TV show you were watching before the phone rang.
- ★ Your watch says fifteen minutes have passed.

CHAPTER ELEVEN
BLABBERMOUTHS!

⑥ *Sunday*

Today my mum was bitten by the cleaning bug and ordered me to clean up my room from top to bottom. It wasn't enough to simply straighten out my desk and gather up all my loose papers, no. She also told me to clean out my closet, where according to her all my junk has been piling up for years. Needless to say, I had no desire to follow her orders and instead had a ball hauling out all this old stuff I didn't even remember I had. Among all the trinkets, I found a picture of mine from a couple of years ago, with me in one of my mum's dresses that I wore for my "shows" in the backyard. I was one funny-looking little kid!

⑥ *Monday*

Days don't come much worse than today! And all because of those

Grumper sisters and their big mouths. It all started when I brought that picture of me to school to show Will and the others. What I didn't want to do, though, was show anyone else, so, during recess I called the girls over to a corner to take a look. But, wouldn't you know it? Those Grumper sisters must be armed with some kind of special radar, because as soon as I pulled out the photo, they suddenly materialized behind us, ogling and laughing and commenting on my silly picture at the tops of their lungs! Now the WHOLE school knows about my horrible outfit. Even the walls know . . . but at least they can't laugh.

⑤ *Tuesday*

Today, searching for a remedy for yesterday's fiasco, we reached the conclusion that the only thing left for me to do is play the situation down.

Well, if they are going to tease me about my ugly outfit, I'll really give them something to sink their teeth into! Going through my things I found the sequined top that my aunt gave me for my birthday last year, which I've never worn. With this on, I'm sure to surprise everyone at school tomorrow!

⑥ *Wednesday*

It worked! As soon as I got to school, people started turning their heads in disbelief. I even went to the boys' basketball practise session wearing the top and the coach yelled at the whole team for missing too many shots, because they were too busy staring at ME!

At recess I saw the Grumper sisters in the hall; they stood there gaping. They were too chicken to say anything, so I did all the talking . . . and thanked them for the free publicity on my great sense of style.

P.S.: Here's another secret that I'll make sure those two blabbermouths never hear: I can't wait till this whole thing blows over. . . . because I'd rather wear trainers than high heels any day!

THE ORACLE SAYS . . .

If someone is telling one of
your secrets, try to explain to her
how bad she would feel if someone
were spreading one of her secrets all over
the place!

Look for support from your closest friends.
It's times like these when real friends will be
there to lend a helping hand. The magic of
friendship at full power helps!

FIVE RESPONSES WHEN SOMEONE HAS FOUND OUT ONE OF YOUR SECRETS

WILL: I congratulate the person: he or she has a future as a private detective!

IRMA: I say something funny in order to come off as cheery and indifferent.

TARANEE: I try to beat the person down . . . with words!

CORNELIA: What secret are you talking about?

HAY LIN: I say nothing at all, in order to give the impression that I really don't care.

CHAPTER TWELVE
OPERATION: SURPRISE PARTY

FROM IRMA'S DIARY

⑥ *Sunday*

At last! Will, Taranee, Hay Lin, and I have come up with a super idea for Cornelia's birthday – a surprise party! The four of us had a meeting this afternoon at my house to make arrangements, but as soon as we sat down to talk about it, the phone rang. It was Cornelia, asking if I wanted to go to the movies. Panic! I made up an excuse and said I had a twenty-four-hour flu. That was a close one! I have the feeling that we're going to have our work cut out for us trying to keep this party a secret!

⑥ *Monday*

This afternoon we met to decide on a place for the party. . . . but we got absolutely nowhere!

Will wanted to have it at her house, but lately her mum's been up to her neck with work, so she's too busy. My house is out, since next Saturday my parents are having friends of theirs over for lunch. Taranee's house is also out, since they're redecorating her living room. "Don't even think about it," was their only reply. Hay Lin's parents' restaurant would be perfect, but it's always full, especially on weekends. But we're not going to give up! Tomorrow we're going to talk to Cornelia's mum about it. . . . IT'S OUR ONLY HOPE!!!

⑥ *Tuesday*

Today we went to Cornelia's (she was at her skating lesson) to ask Mrs. Hale if we could have the party there. We were as polite and kind and sweet as could be. . . . and her mother said yes! This was only, however, after giving us the third

degree: how many kids would there be, what would we be doing, what time did we expect to finish, etc. But in the end, we managed to convince her, after agreeing to a list of solemn promises:

1) We'll make sure the house is as clean as a house in a soap commercial after we're finished.
2) We won't break or destroy anything (fragile objects will be stored away like priceless items in a museum).
3) We won't shatter the neighbors' eardrums with overly loud music.

So we got permission to have the party at Cornelia's house! And that's not all: we also managed to get Mrs. Hale to agree to a NO ADULTS ALLOWED clause!

Wednesday

Today's mission: *find the phone numbers of Cornelia's friends, to invite them to the party.*

This was no problem for the kids at Sheffield, but it was tough locating her older friends. Luckily, I found an ally who knew how to get hold of Corny's old address book . . . on the condition that we invite her to the party, too. Yes, I'm talking about that little snoop of a sister, Lilian, who knows every inch of Cornelia's room by heart! It was work, but in the end I called and sent IMs and e-mails to all her old buddies, telling them to be there this Saturday at 3 P.M. sharp! In the meantime, Taranee made a list of everything we need for the party.

⑥ *Thursday*

Music day . . . We asked all the guests we know best to bring as many CDs as possible.

Hay Lin, our resident art wiz, made a huge Happy Birthday poster, which everyone will sign before Corny shows up, that we're going to hang on the front door. It seems too good to be true, but it looks as though all the preparations are finally in order. . . . one day ahead of schedule! We're great. . . . MAGIC, I would say!

⑥ *Friday*

HELP! Tomorrow's the big day! Let's keep our fingers crossed – especially the part about keeping the party a surprise. We couldn't pretend not to remember it was Corny's birthday, or she would have known something was up. Luckily, Peter offered to give us a hand: he'll give her a ride home while we take care of the final details.

And now . . . let me relax a little and think about an even bigger problem – what to wear tomorrow!

⑥ *Saturday*

The party was a hit!! You should have seen Cornelia. She hardly had time to open her mouth before we all started cheering and tossing confetti . . . and the party began! A truly GREAT afternoon! On Monday at school we won't be talking about anything else!

WHAT YOU CAN DO IF . . .

You can't find a place for your surprise party.

- Try to think of someone you know who has a garage or an attic that you could use.
- Weather permitting, have it in a park. All you need is a lawn and some old blankets for a picnic. Just remember to clean everything up before leaving!

You're having a party with only four to six guests.

- Make it a sleepover dance party: bring music, pajamas, and sleeping bags, and you can dance and talk all night long!
- Make it a movie marathon: rent all the videos with your favourite star that you can find, load up on popcorn and soda, take over the TV room, and . . . ACTION!
- Make it a special dinner party: have fun cooking together, and try some new recipes.

You're arranging a surprise party for a friend, but don't know how to keep the surprise from her.

● Drag her shopping with you because you "absolutely have to" show her where the cutest clerk in town works.

● Convince her to come to a friend's house to copy some excellent history notes.

● Tell her you're feeling a little down, and invite her for some ice-cream therapy.

DEAR WILL
Will is a good leader and advice-giver!

Dear Will,
My friends are planning a surprise party for me,
but I've found out everything. What can I do?
– Party Pooper

Dear Party Pooper,
How about a performance worthy of an
Oscar nomination for Best Surprised
Birthday Girl?
 Will

Dear Will,
I forgot to bake a cake for a party. Is it really
necessary?
– Cakeless

Dear Cakeless,
You can always substitute something just as
scrumptious. . . . Why not try birthday cookies?
 Will

CHAPTER THIRTEEN
CODES FOR ALL TASTES

FROM IRMA'S DIARY

🌀 *Tuesday*

If there were a contest, I'd win First Prize for putting my foot in my mouth!

This morning I wrote a note to Hay Lin to tell her that I had gone out with Martin (we went to the museum to check out the beetle collection – YUCK!). But our old eagle-eyed science teacher intercepted the message and read it out loud in front of the whole class. She said that that way everyone would appreciate my "remarkable interest in natural sciences."

Now half the school is sniggering behind my back about my "interest" in . . . Martin!

◎ *Wednesday*

Today at the park I talked with my friends about what happened yesterday in class. We've decided to make up a secret language that only we can understand . . . a secret code for every occasion!

I'm writing the translations below so I don't forget them – like Will forgot the password for her computer. (She had to clean her whole room just to find the slip of paper she'd written it on – it was under her dormouse's pillow!)

NUMERICAL ALPHABET

For top-secret messages that even your math teacher won't be able to figure out!

Each letter of the alphabet corresponds to a number:

A=26, B=25, C=24, D=23, E=22, and so on.

For example: **"Today I'm happy"** becomes:

Today = 7-12-23-26-2

I'm = 18-14

happy = 19-26-11-11-2

SHORT AND SWEET

Use these code letters in the presence of anyone with a "wandering eye."

KIT	Keep In Touch
NP	No Problem
BBL	Be Back Later
SYS	See You Soon
TOY	Thinking Of You
BF	Boyfriend
HCM!	He Called Me!
CYL	Call You Later
HB	Happy Birthday
DYR?	Do You Remember?

INSTANT MESSAGE CODES

For quick and easy communication

:-)	I'm happy
:-))	I'm ecstatic
:-(	I'm sad
:-((	I'm down in the dumps
%-)	I'm confused
:-S	I don't know what to say
:-/	I'm undecided
:-?	I don't understand
=)	I blushed
=S	I'm nervous
:°(	I'm crying
>:-(	I'm mad
:-@	What a blast
:-C	How's it going?
:-I	Fantastic
(:-#	Keep your lips sealed
:-*	A kiss
^@*	I'm head over heels in love
:-[	He made me mad
I-O	I'm tired
:->	I really dig him
6@	You're my love
-=	I bombed out on the test

-*)=	I did great on the test
#-	I have to stay home
:-9	I can't wait
+!	Okay!
-!	I wouldn't dream of it
W!	Set plan into motion!
:-**ZZZZ**	What a drag!

OPPOSITES

Use this system when some busybody is listening in on your conversation. But remember, before "activating" the system, make sure you and your friend each know what the other is talking about!

I don't like him.
I really dig him.

I know my history backward and forward.
If there's a geography quiz I'm sunk.

I don't feel like going out today.
See you at the usual spot.

I'm spending the entire afternoon studying.
Let's hit the stores for some big-time shopping.

I haven't heard from him in ages.
He called me yesterday.

I don't like sending e-mails.
I just got an e-mail.

Bummer, no party.
We're invited to the party.

I haven't heard that song in a while.
Let's find a way to make it to the concert.

He looks like a swamp beast on a bad day.
What a hunk!

SECRET ALPHABET
For longer secret messages

A = .		N = !
B = ,		O = "
C = ;		P = -
D = Y		Q = +
E = ı		R =)
F = <		S = (
G = À		T = ~
H = È		U = . . .
I = :		V = ^
J = @		W = %
K = #		X = &
L = '		Y = /
M = ?		Z = Æ

For example: **"See you at 5 p.m."** =
(ı ı /". . . ~ 5-?

DRESS THE WAY YOU FEEL

To avoid questions like "How are you?"

White = I'm cool.
Red = Don't rub me the wrong way.
Yellow = Beware of gossip.
Blue = I'm your friend.
Green = I feel on top of the world.
Lilac = My head is in the clouds.
Orange = I need a vacation.
Gray = I didn't study.
Pink = Everything went smoothly!
Light blue = Do you want to go out this
afternoon?

IRMA'S TIPS

Having a secret language means . . .

- Speaking to and being understood by only certain people.
- Making my secrets even more secret.
- Having fun with my friends.
- Having a language all my own.
- Coming up with the most absurd combinations and having a barrel of laughs with friends.
- Keeping busybodies out of my world.
- Keeping our group united.

TEST

Can you keep a secret?

Begin with Question #1, then add up the points and discover your true secret-keeping nature.

1. You're the first to catch a glimpse of some test results in class. One of your friends passed with flying colours, but another failed. When the two of them come up to you after school . . .
   A. You manage to speak to each of them in private, first one, then the other.
   B. You immediately blurt out the news to both of them at the same time.

2. In class the kids are all wondering why two of your friends have stopped talking to each other. You know the reason . . .
   A. But your lips are sealed – after all, it's none of their business.
   B. So you spill the beans.

3. There's a gossip queen spreading rumours left and right. You . . .
   A. Unmask her in public.

B. Secretly inform everyone you know about the situation.

4. Your brother decides to do something you think is wrong. Would you tell your parents?
   A. No.
   B. It depends.

5. You know that lately a friend of yours can't stand another one of your friends. One of the two friends asks you if you're aware of the situation. Do you tell her the truth?
   A. Only if you want to create more friction.
   B. You tell her you hadn't realised.

6. One of your friends tells you a secret.
   A. You're somewhat embarrassed. You feel that she shouldn't have told you.
   B. Satisfied, you run to tell your classmates, the janitor, and your third cousin.

PROFILES

Points:	A	B	Points:	A	B
1.	1	2	4.	1	2
2.	1	2	5.	2	1
3.	2	1	6.	1	2

Profile A (0–3)

Mum's the Word

You know all the ins and outs of keeping a secret. You're 100 percent reliable and wouldn't crack even under torture. You're convinced that a secret is a secret only when there's just one person who knows it, and you become suspicious even when it is shared with you. You're the ideal confidant.

Profile B (4–6)

Secret Agent

Secret-keeping is your job. If you so decide, a secret will forever stay a secret with you, but only if you alone make that decision. You're careful and you're a great observer – nothing escapes your gaze. Once you've decided to keep a secret, no one can get in your way – you easily come up with excuses for not giving the secret away. You assess each secret with great skill, and you are in command of every situation!

Profile C (7–9)
Apprentice

No, you're not inclined to gossip. You know how to keep a secret, as long as the person who tells you first asks you to keep silent. You may tend to run off at the mouth, but not out of meanness. These little slipups may indicate that you've got some problems managing your own secrets. Keep practicing the fine art of keeping a secret, and don't worry – you'll learn quick enough!

Profile D (10–12)
The Daily Blab

Secret? Did I hear a secret? Anybody got a secret? Not anymore . . . You love nothing more than spilling the beans, telling everyone everything every time, and you see nothing wrong with that. The important thing is to have fun, right? As soon as you find out something juicy, you divulge it. With your talent, you should consider a career in journalism, although your friends should definitely think twice before letting you in on their secrets.